On Becoming Teenwise

FLY GUY PRESENTS:

FIREFIGHTERS

Tedd Arnold

Scholastic Inc.

For Mikel, Jakob, and Ayden,
with a salute to Uncle Mikel, volunteer
firefighter extraordinaire! —T.A.

Photos ©: cover: Rob Wilson/Shutterstock, Inc.; cover: Leelakajonkij/Shutterstock, Inc.; back cover: MarkCoffeyPhoto/iStockphoto; 4 –5: Ian Dagnall/Alamy Images; 6 –7: Purestoc /Alamy Images; 7: Jon Rile/Getty Images; 8 left: thelinke/iStockphoto; 8 right: Carsten Reisinger/Shutterstock, Inc.; 9: Bob Winsett/Getty Images; 10 center right: MedicImage/Getty Images; 10 top: National Geographic Image Collection/Alamy Images; 10 center left: IPaul Matthew Photography; 10 bottom right: Jens Molin/Shutterstock, Inc.; 11 bottom: Monkey Business Images/Shutterstock, Inc.; 11 and throughout–burn holes: NRT/Shutterstock, Inc.; 11 top: Chantal de Bruijne/Shutterstock, Inc.; 11 and throughout–burn marks: nrt/Shutterstock, Inc.; 12 bottom: ML Harris/Getty Images; 12 top: Jonathan Lesage/Getty Images; 1 2 –13 background: Hefr/Shutterstock, Inc.; 13: Flashon Studio/Shutterstock, Inc.; 14: JSAbbott/iStockphoto; 15 bottom right: Gabbro/ Alamy Images; 15 top: Bettmann/Corbis Images; 15 bottom left: Photo Collection of Alexander Alland, Sr./Corbis Images; 16 bottom: Matthew Strauss/911 Pictures; 16 top: TFoxFoto; 17 bottom: Joshua Corsa/911 Pictures; 17 center: Mishela/Shutterstock, Inc.; 18: Bill Stormont/Alamy Images; 19 top: moodboard/Getty Images; 19 center: Photolibrary/Getty Images; 20: Alan Schein Photography/Corbis Images; 21 bottom: Peter Casolino/Alamy Images; 21 top: MarkCoffeyPhoto/iStockphoto; 22: Najlah Feanny/Corbis SABA; 23 bottom: The Orange County Register, Stuart Palley/AP Images; 23 top: Rafael Marchante/Reuters; 24 top: Jeff Thrower/Shutterstock, Inc.; 25 bottom: Churck Berman/Chicago Tribumt/MCY via Getty Images; 25 top: Charles Schug/iStockphoto; 26 top: Popular Science/Getty Images; 26 center: Erin Tracy/Modesto Bee/Zuma Press; 27 top: Amy Walters/Shutterstock, Inc.; 27 center: Fotostory/Shutterstock, Inc.; 28 bottom: Chris Trotman/Getty Images for NASCAR; 28 right: Art Directors & TRIP/Alamy Images; 28 left: Tadeusz Ibrom/ Shutterstock, Inc.; 29 bottom: Gilles Mingasson/Getty Images; 29 top: worradirek/Shutterstock, Inc.; 30 top left: Kris Timken/Getty Images; 30 center: Kris Timken/Getty Images; 30 top right: Monkey Business Images/Shutterstock, Inc.

ISBN 978-0-545-63160-0

12 11 10 9 8 7 6 5 4 3 2 1   14 15 16 17 18/0

Printed in the U.S.A.   40
First printing, August 2014

A boy had a pet fly named Fly Guy.
Fly Guy could say the boy's name —

"I am SO-O-O excited to go to the fire station!" said Buzz.

Fly Guy looked scared.

FIREZZZ?

"Don't worry!" said Buzz. "There's no fire inside. A fire station is where we'll find firefighters and fire trucks."

Buzz and Fly Guy wanted to learn more.

In the fire station, Fly Guy and Buzz met the fire chief. A fire chief is a firefighter who is in charge of the station.

He gets a call when someone pulls a fire alarm or dials 9-1-1.

The fire chief learns what and where the emergency (ee-MUR-juhn-see) is. Then an alarm sounds at the station.

RESCUE CENTER

ALARM

Firefighters need to move fast!

The firefighters rush to their trucks!
Sometimes they slide down a fire pole.
This is a fast way for firefighters to get
to the garage.

Fire trucks are parked in the engine bay, or garage.

Each truck has special equipment (ee-KWIP-muhnt) that is used to put out fires.

rope

fire ax

fire extinguisher

The trucks are always ready so that firefighters can race to the scene.

WE'RE ON OUR WAY.

Firefighters keep their gear in the garage next to their trucks. It protects them and helps them to do their job.

When there's an emergency, firefighters have to get dressed fast. They put on their gear in less than one minute!

HELMET PROTECTS FROM FALLING OBJECTS

SPECIAL MASK HELPS WITH BREATHING AND SEEING IN SMOKE

OXYGEN TANK

FIREPROOF GLOVES

FIREPROOF PANTS

FIREPROOF AND WATERPROOF BOOTS

All that gear weighs about 50 pounds!

A fire truck needs to get to the fire fast so that firefighters can put it out, or extinguish (eks-TIHN-gwish) it.

Fire trucks have loud sirens and flashing lights to warn other drivers that the fire truck is speeding through.

Long ago, firefighters
did not have trucks. Firefighters, horses,
or even fire dogs pulled a pump and hose
on a big cart.

There is a pump panel inside each truck. It controls the hoses.

pump panel

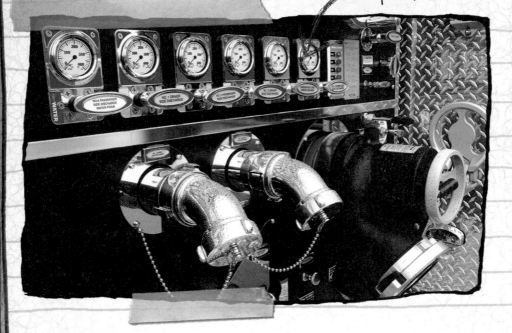

Every truck has a long hose and a tank filled with about 25 bathtubs full of water.

hose

Pumps push water through the hose at 1,000 gallons per minute.

If the water runs out, firefighters can hook up their hoses to fire hydrants.

Firefighters carry lots of extra tools to use in an emergency. Ladders and axes can help them reach someone trapped in a burning building.

Firefighters have lots of skills.

Many firefighters have some medical training. They carry first-aid kits to help people who are hurt.

Each fire truck has a tall ladder on top. The ladder extends and helps firefighters rescue people in tall buildings.

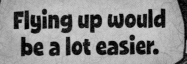

Flying up would be a lot easier.

YEZZZ!

The ladders can reach 100 feet up. That's about as tall as five giraffes stacked on top of each other!

Firefighters use fire-rescue boats to put out fires on the water.

Fireboats to the rescue!

They fight fires from oil spills and fires on other boats.

For a large fire, like a forest fire, firefighters use helicopters.

helicopter

Water and special firefighting chemicals are poured onto the flames below.

Firefighters don't just put out fires. They sometimes rescue people and animals from other dangers like car accidents, blizzards, and floods.

CAR RESCUE

Being a firefighter is an important and dangerous job.

ICE RESCUE

HEROZZ

FLOOD RESCUE

Many firefighters are volunteers. That means they do not get paid. They volunteer to help keep their communities safe.

It's not just firefighters that save lives. Some fire stations have specially trained fire-rescue dogs! They help people who are trapped or injured in a fire.

Hey, fella!

Fire-rescue dogs
wear extra gear, too.

Firefighters help keep people safe. But they have to stay safe, too!

That's why they practice for all kinds of emergencies. They call these practice sessions drills.

drills

In safe areas they learn how to extinguish fires.

Putting out a fire!

Firefighters train and exercise, so they can move quickly in dangerous situations.

EXERCIZZZE!

CLASS FIRE DRILL

Fire drills are important, and not just for firefighters. Everyone should be ready for an emergency. Most fires are started by accident.

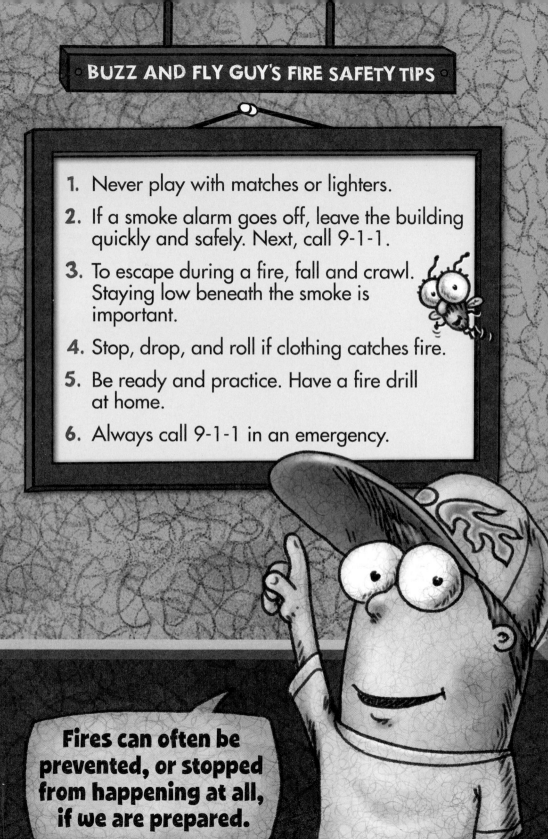

"Firefighters have an amazing job!" Buzz said. "It is so cool that they help so many people and keep us safe."

Buzz and Fly Guy cannot wait to go on another field trip!

FLY GUY PRESENTS

Go on field trips with Fly Guy!

A non-fiction series filled with fun facts and cool photos!

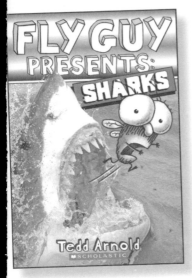

Follow Fly Guy to the aquarium to learn all about sharks!

"A first-rate sharkfest."
—*Kirkus Reviews*

Follow Fly Guy to the space museum to learn all about space!

Follow Fly Guy to the natural history museum to learn all about dinosaurs!

Available in print and eBook editions

scholastic.com/flyguy

FGPRES3

Fly Guy is buzzing over to the firehouse today. Come along to learn all about firefighters!

BOOKZZZ!

APPEALS TO
K-2ND GRADERS

READING LEVEL
GRADE 2

$3.99 US / $4.99 C

SCHOLASTIC
www.scholastic.com

ISBN 978-0-545-63160-0

More leveling information for this book:
www.scholastic.com/readinglevel

09-CDP-103